Voices for Safety

AF859920

The Subscription *Trap*

A Consumer's Survival Guide

Written by: Wendy Busse-Coleman

Copyright © 2026 Wendy Busse-Coleman
All rights reserved.
Published by Wendy Busse-Coleman
ISBN 978-1-105-02155-8

For more resources, updates, and companion tools, visit:
https://www.voicesforsafety.com

Dedication

For every consumer who has ever felt tricked, trapped, or talked over.

For the people who were told *"that's just how it works,"* even when it wasn't fair.
For anyone who has spent hours trying to cancel something that should have taken minutes.

This book is for you -
for your time, your money, your voice,
and your right to clarity in a world that profits from confusion.

May you always speak louder than the chaos.

Wendy Busse-Coleman

Founder, Content Creator, Blogger,
and Virtual Visionary

What's Inside

Intentionally Blank

Why I Built This Book

This book kicked off the instant I had an epiphany: modern companies' customer service was as off-kilter as a wobbly table!

It's not just the odd surprise renewal or a baffling cancellation maze; it's a whole circus of confusion and hush-hush tactics! A setup where consumers' wallets whisper a sad goodbye each month, while corporations laugh all the way to the bank.

I didn't set out to write a book.

I set out to understand why everyday people were being trapped by subscriptions they didn't remember signing up for, couldn't easily cancel, or never meant to keep. And the deeper I went, the clearer the truth became:

the subscription economy is designed to benefit from your forgetfulness, your frustration, and your time.

I crafted this book because folks deserve crystal-clear answers. They need the right tools, the perfect words, and a big boost of confidence. They have every right to know the ins and outs of the system and how to give it a nudge when it turns pesky!

I immersed myself in consumer protection and technology to help people navigate the digital marketplace. I created tools like **Subscription Watch**™ for tracking spending on subscriptions and the difficult cancellations. This book serves as a comprehensive guide, compiling all that knowledge in one convenient package!

This book isn't just a collection of facts; it's a superhero cape of empowerment! It's your trusty flashlight in pitch-black corridors and a treasure map through the twisty, turny maze of life that was never meant to be a stroll in the park.

If you've ever felt tricked, trapped, or ignored by a subscription company, this book is for you. And, if you've ever wished someone would finally explain how to fight back... that's why I built it.

The Mission That Drives Me

I'm your friendly neighborhood consumer-protection crusader and the genius behind ***Subscription Watch***™. This nifty digital sidekick helps folks like you keep tabs on subscriptions, tackle the sticky mess of cancellation woes, and stand up to those pesky, sneaky tricks in the wild world of commerce!

I'm on a mission, armed with a keyboard and a megaphone, to help folks navigate the digital jungle that's as clear as mud! Through my brainchild, ***Voices for Safety***(tm), I whip up research, and educational goodies to empower people. Together, we'll crack the code of your rights, spot those sneaky dark patterns, and give a firm nudge when companies try to trap you in their sticky web!

The ***Subscription Trap*** is your cheerful companion through the maze of crafty subscriptions. If you've ever felt tricked or caught in the cycle of a subscription service, this is your way out! I'm convinced you deserve clarity, fairness, and a handy toolkit to reclaim control.

My mission? To ensure you have all this and more, with a smile!

Thank You!
Wendy

Introduction

You're Already Paying for Something You Forgot About

Let me say something that most people don't want to admit: right now, at this exact moment, you are probably paying for at least one subscription you completely forgot about. Maybe two. Could be five.

I've been exploring this topic for quite some time, and while I may not be a tech expert or a financial whiz, I'm a 66-year-old woman from Maryland who's had enough of companies using the fine print as their secret stash and making the *Cancel Button* a challenge! I've shared my thoughts on this often because I believe in creating positive change. After all, who doesn't love a wonderful life transformation, right?

This guidebook is what I wish existed ten years ago. It's not academic. It's not full of legal jargon. It's written the way I talk to a friend: directly, honestly and with zero patience for nonsense.

What You'll Walk Away With

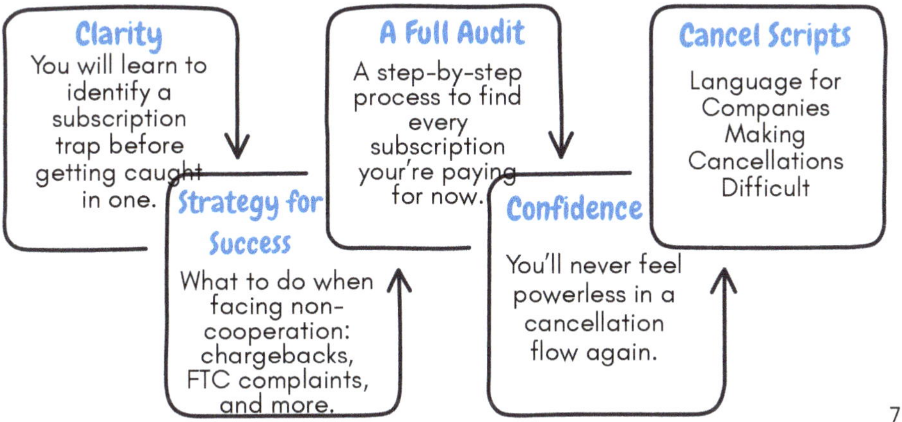

Intentionally Blank

(1) What Is a Subscription Trap?

Understanding the Problem Before You Can Solve It

Welcome to the world of subscription traps, where signing up is as easy as pie, but breaking free is like escaping quicksand! It's not always against the rules, and it's sneakier than a cat burglar, but let's face it—99.9% of the time, it's as intentional as a cat knocking over a glass of water!

There is a range of subscription service experiences, from companies that fail to remind you when your trial ends to those companies that take your money for months, complicate cancellation by hiding contact information and requiring a survey just to find the cancel button.

The Three Zones of a Subscription Trap

ZONE 1 THE SETUP

The moment you hand over your payment info. This is where companies collect what they need. Free Trials, 'Risk-Free' Offers, and Introductory Pricing are all tactics

ZONE 2 THE DRIFT

The period where charges happen quietly. You're busy. Life is loud. $12.99 slides through every month and you don't notice, or, you notice but tell yourself you'll deal with it later.

ZONE 3 THE TRAP

When attempting to leave, you encounter 'dark patterns' like confusing cancellation processes, guilt-inducing retention scripts, and continued billing despite perceived cancellation.

Intentionally Blank

(2) The 8 Dark Patterns They Use

Name Them. Spot Them. Refuse Them.

A "dark pattern" is like a sneaky ninja in the digital world, crafted to bamboozle, hoodwink, or nudge you into decisions that might not be what you really want.

Get ready to uncover the top 8 tricksters lurking in subscription land over the next two pages!

DARK PATTERN: THE ROACH MOTEL

What it is: Easy to check in, Impossible to check out.

How to spot it: One-click sign-up with 6-step cancellation. The cancel option is buried in Settings > Account > Billing > Manage Plan > Downgrade > Cancel.

How to fight back: Document every step with screenshots. If cancellation takes more steps than to sign-up, report it to the FTC.

DARK PATTERN: THE CONFIRM-SHAMING BUTTON

What it is: Making you feel bad for wanting to leave..

How to spot it: Cancel buttons labeled 'No thanks, I don't want to save money' or 'I'll pay full price instead.' Designed to trigger shame and second-guessing.

How to fight back: Ignore the emotional language. Click whatever button stops the charge. You don't owe them guilt.

The 8 Dark Patterns They Use

THE HIDDEN RENEWAL

What it is: Burying the auto-renewal clause where you don't find it..

How to spot it: Sign-up page promotes the law first price in LARGE FONT. Auto-Renewal at full price is in font size-8 gray text below the fold.

How to fight back: Before you subscribe, scroll all the way down. Search the page for 'renew', 'automatic', and 'cancel' to find the real terms.

THE FORCED CONTINUITY

What it is: Charging your form of payment after a free trial without a clear 'friendly' reminder.

How to spot it: No email the day or more before the trial ends. Charge appears 24 hours after trial, often on a weekend or holiday.

How to fight back: Set a calendar alert for 2 days before your trial ends. Always, Every time. No exceptions.

THE SAVE / PAUSE TRAP

What it is: Offering a 'pause' when you ask to cancel.

How to spot it: You ask to cancel. They offer 3 FREE months or a pause. You accept. Charges resume automatically and you forget.

How to fight back: If you want to CANCEL, say "I want to FULLY cancel my account and stop ALL future charges." DO NOT accept pauses unless you actively want them.

The 8 Dark Patterns They Use

THE PHANTOM RETENTION TEAM

What it is: Routing you to a 'retention specialist' who has 30 minutes to change your mind.

How to spot it: Cancel requires a phone call. You're on hold for 20 minutes, then transferred to someone trained specifically to keep you subscribing.

How to fight back: Before calling, write down this phrase: "I am cancelling today. I do not want any offers. Please confirm my cancellation number.' Repeat it.

THE IMPOSSIBLE PHONE NUMBER

What it is: Hiding the cancellation phone number or making it unavailable.

How to spot it: Website shows no customer service number. Chat bot loops endlessly. Email gets auto-replies. The only way out is a number that doesn't appear on the site.

How to fight back: Consider using Copilot Chat by providing the company name and requesting information on "how to reach out via telephone to cancel." This has been my reliable method for this sitution. Or, Google or check Yelp reviews for tips.

THE SNEAK-IN CHARGE

What it is: Adding a product or upgrade to your cart without asking.

How to spot it: Checkout page pre-checks an add-on, insurance, or renewal. You don't notice and pay for something you never intended to buy.

How to fight back: Slow down at checkout. Read every line. Uncheck everything that wasn't your explicit choice. If you were charged for something you didn't choose, that may be illegal.

Subscription Watch (tm) - Your Companion Tool for Fighting *Subscription Friction*

Introducing **Subscription Watch**, your trusty sidekick in taming the wild jungle of digital subscriptions! This nifty gizmo keeps your digital life on a tight leash, helping both you and me to:

- Keep tabs on every subscription lurking in your life
- Score the drama level of each company's cancellation circus
- Capture the sneaky dark-pattern tricks
- Fire off FTC complaints with Subscription Watch
- Stash your evidence in your trusty 'vault'
- Maintain a tidy, detective-style dossier on what you're paying for and why

If you want a simple way to stay ahead of surprise renewals, cancellation traps, and deceptive free trials, **Subscription Watch** (tm) is designed for you.

FREE for Book Owners!

As a "thank you" for diving into "**The Subscription Trap**," every reader gets a VIP pass to **Subscription Watch** absolutely free!

subscription
WATCH™
Your Subscription Radar

This book teaches you how to avoid subscription traps. Subscription Watch (tm) helps you stay out of them.

Your purchase unlocks both.

Instructions for redeeming your FREE access are included at the end of the Appendix.

(3) The Subscription Audit

Know What You're Paying - All of it

This is the single most important thing you can do in the next 30 minutes. A ***subscription audit*** is a systematic search for every recurring charge leaving your accounts. Most people find at least one they forgot about. Many find three or four.

1. **Pull your bank and credit card statements**

Go back 90 days. Look for any charge that appears more than once. Amount doesn't matter... $1.99 and $299.99 both count. Write down the company name and amount for every repeat charge.

2. **Check your email for subscription confirmations**

Search your inbox for: 'YOUR SUBSCRIPTION', 'TRIAL STARTED', 'PAYMENT CONFIRMED', 'INVOICE', AND 'RECEIPT'. Go back as far as you can. You may find services you signed up for years ago.

3. **Check your app store subscriptions**

APPLE: Settings > [YOUR NAME] > Subscriptions. **GOOGLE PLAY**: Play Store > Account > Subscriptions. Both show active and recently expired subscriptions you may have forgotten.

4. **Check PayPal, Venmo, Zelle**

Go to Settings > Automatic Payments or Recurring Payments in each service. Companies sometimes route charges through PayPal so they don't appear on your card statement.

5. **Ask yourself the hard question**

For each subscription you find: *Have I used this in the last 30 days?* If no, *do I plan to use it in the next 30 days?* **If the answer is NO twice, cancel today. Right now. Don't put it off.**

The Subscription Audit

What to Track for Each Subscription

WHAT TO TRACK	WHY IT MATTERS
Service/Subscription Name and URL	You'll need the exact URL to find the CANCEL page later
Monthly/Annual Amount	So you know EXACTLY how much you'll save when you CANCEL
Billing Date	Gives you the dealine... CANCEL BEFORE this date to avoid the next charge
Trial End Date (if applicable)	The most important date... This is when the CHARGE starts
How You Signed Up	Email, Facebook Login, Google Login... Affects how you CANCEL
Cancellation Method	Phone, Online, Email or Chat... Know what you are walking into
Cancellation CONFIRMATION #	Proof the CANCELLATION happened... Always get this or the confirming email from the company

> 42% of people say a "free trial" turned into a paid subscription without their clear consent.

Now That You Know What You're Paying For...

If you want help organizing your subscriptions, tracking renewal dates, and documenting cancellation friction, I built a tool for exactly that.

subscription
WATCH™
Your Subscription Radar

This nifty web app is your trusty sidekick for logging every subscription, rating the escape difficulty level, and dodging those sneaky surprise charges. It's your post-audit superhero, ensuring you never tumble into the subscription trap again!

The trap ends here.

Intentionally Blank

Even When They Make It Hard

Here is the truth that no one tells you:

you have the right to cancel any subscription at any time. The company does not get to decide if your reason is good enough. They do not get to talk you out of it. Your money, your choice.

The Universal Cancel Script

For phone calls: "I am calling to cancel my account effective today, I do not want any retention offers, upgrades, or pauses. I want a full cancellation and a confirmation number. Please confirm my account is cancelled. And follow-up with an email to: *[REPEAT YOUR EMAIL ADDRESS]*.

For online chat: "I need to cancel my account effective today. Please do not offer alternatives. Confirm cancellation in this chat window and provide a confirmation number. And follow-up with an email to: *[PROVIDE YOUR EMAIL ADDRESS]*.

For email: "I am writing to cancel my *[SERVICE/SUBSCRIPTION NAME]* account, email *[INCLUDE YOUR EMAIL ADDRESS]*, effective immediately. Please confirm cancellation and that no further charges will occur. I want a written confirmation of this cancellation."

"You're not the problem. The system is."

Cancellation Methods by Difficulty

How to Cancel Anything

ONLINE SELF-SERVICE	**Easiest**	Go to Account > Settings > Billing > Cancel. If you can't find it, try Ctrl +F or Command +F and search for 'cancel' on the page
LIVE CHAT	**Medium**	Keep a transcript of the CHAT. Screenshot the confirmation. If they say "it's been processed," ask for a Confirmation Number before you close the window.
PHONE CALL	**Hard**	Record the call if your state allows it (check first - many do). Write down the time, date, representative's name, and confirmation number.
CERTIFIED MAIL	**Nuclear Option**	For companies that have ignored everything else send a certified letter to their billing address stating you are CANCELLING, effective the date of the letter. Keep the USPS tracking receipt. This creates a legal paper trail

Want to shine a spotlight on tricky cancellation tactics, track the hassle factor, and hold companies accountable for playing hard to get? Enter **Subscription Watch**™—your trusty sidekick in the battle against subscription shenanigans!

It records the nitty-gritty of your cancellation saga, serves up FTC complaint links on a silver platter, and lets you shout above the noise. Make it your go-to buddy whenever a company tries to trap you in their web.

The pièce de resistance? The ***CANCELLATION GRADE***! Answer a few questions about your cancellation escapade, and **Subscription Watch**™ scores it from A to F. If you land in D, E, or F territory, it'll nudge you to submit a complaint to the FTC. It's a breeze to zoom from the app to FTC-land, with handy templates galore—or go freestyle with your own words when you reach the FTC site.

More than 70% of consumers feel frustrated or stressed when trying to cancel a subscription.

Intentionally Blank

Unleash Your Inner Superhero with What You've Got!

If you've jumped through all the hoops and they're still billing you, or playing hide-and-seek with your cancellation, fear not! You're armed with real options. These aren't just desperate measures these are your superstar consumer rights that most folks don't even realize they possess!

1. **Dispute the charge with your bank or credit card**

This is call a 'chargeback.' Call your card issuer and say: "I cancelled this subscription on [DATE] and they charged me. I would like to dispute these charges." Most banks will credit you within 5 - 7 business days and investigate the merchant. You typically have 60-120 days from the charge date to file a dispute.

2. **File a complaint with the FTC**

Go to **reportfraud.ftc.gov.** This takes about 5 minutes. Your complaint goes into a database that the FTC uses to identify patterns and bring enforcement actions. A single complaint rarely triggers action but a hundred from the same company does.

3. **File with your state attorney general**

Every state has a consumer protection office. Many are more responsive than the FTC for individual cases. Search '[YOUR STATE] attorney general consumer complaint'

> "The subscription economy profits from your silence."

Unleash Your Inner Superhero with What You've Got!

4. **Leave a detailed public review**

A clear, factual, dated review on Google, Yelp, or Trustpilot describing your cancellation experience helps other consumers and often prompts companies to respond and resolve issues to protect their public reputation.

5. **Contact your credit card company about a recurring block**

Ask your card issuer to block future charges from a specific merchant. Most banks can do this. It's a nuclear option, but effective if a company keeps charging after cancellation.

KEEP YOUR EVIDENCE. Before you dispute anything, screenshot or print:

- Your cancellation confirmation
- Your bank statement showing the charges
- Any chat transcripts or emails

Evidence makes every dispute faster and more successful.

"Speak louder than the chaos."

The Lightning-Fast Safety Check That Shields You Every Time!

Now that you're aware of these hidden traps, here's a helpful cheat sheet to review before sharing your payment info for any subscription service. These quick questions can save you from potential headaches later!

[ ] Is there a FREE trial?

If yes: When does it end? Set a calendar reminder for 2 days before.

[ ] What's the deal with the CANCELLATION method?

Do you just click your way out online, or are you destined for an awkward phone chat? If it's phone-only, consider that a yellow flag waving!

[ ]"Where's the CANCEL BUTTON?"

Before signing up, make it your mission to spot it within 30 seconds. If it's playing hide and seek, approach with ninja-level caution! 🕵️

[ ] What's the deal with refunds?

Dive into the Help Center or scour the terms for 'refund.' Legit services lay out their refund policy like an open book!

[ ] Is this charge pre-authorized?

Will they notify you before charging? If not, set your own reminder.

[ ] Have I used a service like this before?

If you cancelled a similar service in the past year, ask yourself honestly why this will be different.

[ ] Do I need this, or do I just want it right now?

The 24-hour rule: If you're not sure, wait one day. Most impulse subscriptions feel less urgent tomorrow.

[ ] Am I using a virtual card number?

Services like PRIVACY.com let you create a card number for one specific merchant with a spending limit. Ideal for trials.

Intentionally Blank

Disclaimer

The tools and services listed in this chapter are provided for informational and educational purposes only. They are included because they may be helpful to consumers navigating subscription management, cancellation barriers, or financial disputes. I do not own, operate, or control these services, and their inclusion does not constitute endorsement, guarantee, or professional recommendation.

Readers are encouraged to assess each resource individually to ascertain its alignment with their personal needs, comfort levels, and privacy expectations. It is important to note that features, pricing, and policies may evolve over time, and availability may differ by region.

Use these tools at your own discretion. This chapter is designed to empower you with options not to direct you toward any specific service.

Why This Chapter Matters

Modern subscription traps thrive because consumers often don't know where to turn for help, how to report deceptive practices, or what tools exist to protect them. This chapter brings all of those resources together in one place. Clear, simple and ready to use.

Whether you're on a mission to audit your subscriptions, battling the dreaded cancellation hurdles, or dodging future snares, these trusty tools have your back every step of the way!

⭐ Federal & Consumer Protection Agencies

Federal Trade Commission (FTC)

The FTC is the primary agency responsible for protecting consumers from unfair or deceptive business practices.

Use the FTC Complaint Assistant when a company:

- Makes cancellation difficult
- Hides fees or renewal terms
- Uses dark patterns
- Charges you after you cancel

Website: ftc.gov

Best For: Reporting deceptive subscription practices.

Consumer Financial Protection Bureau (CFPB)

The CFPB handles financial complaints, including unauthorized charges, surprise renewals, and billing issues.

Use the CFPB portal when:

- You've been charged without consent
- A subscription renewed without notice
- A company refuses to refund an unauthorized charge

Website: consumerfinance.gov

Best For: Billing disputes and financial harm

"You deserve clarity, not confusion."

⭐ Digital Tools for Subscription Safety

PRIVACY.COM

A powerful prevention tool that lets you create virtual payment cards with spending limits, single-use settings, or merchant locks.

Use PRIVACY.com when:

- Signing up for free trials
- Testing new services
- Avoiding surprise renewals
- Protecting your real card information

Best For: **Preventing future subscription traps.**

DoNotPay

A legal-automation service that helps you cancel subscriptions, request refunds, generate complaint letters, and dispute charges.

Use DoNotPay when:

- You want automated cancellation
- You need a quick dispute letter
- You want help filing complaints

Best For: **Readers who prefer automation**

Billshark

A negotiation service that lowers bills and cancels subscriptions on your behalf.

Use Billshark when:

- You want someone else to handle the hassle
- You need help lowering recurring bills
- You want convenience over DIY

Best For: **Saving money without doing the work**

⭐ Your Companion Tool: Subscription Watch™ (Free for Readers)

Subscription Watch is the tool I built to support everything in this book. It helps you:

- Track every subscription
- Rate cancellation friction
- Document dark patterns
- Generate FTC complaint links
- Stay ahead of surprise renewals
- Keep a clean, organized record of what you pay

Every purchaser of **"The Subscription Trap"** receives **full access free.**

This book teaches you how to avoid traps. Subscription Watch **helps you stay out of them.**

Instructions for redeeming your free access appear at the end of the Appendix.

> Automatic renewal is responsible for billions in consumer losses every year.

Why Subscription Watch is Different

the subscription app

that doesn't spy on you

Picture this: most subscription tracking apps are like sneaky little detectives. They cozy up to your email inbox, peek into your bank account, or both! They sift through your private chats, scrutinize your shopping sprees, and keep tabs on your financial escapades to spot those pesky subscriptions.

Convenient? Sure. But it comes with a price: your privacy!

Subscription Watch™ was built to be the opposite.

Privacy First — Always

We do not:

- read your emails
- scan your inbox for receipts
- monitor your bank account
- analyze your spending
- track your purchases
- scrape your financial data

We don't believe you should have to trade your privacy for convenience. Not today. Not ever.

What We Do Instead

Subscription Watch gives you **intentional control:**

- You enter your subscription manually.
- We automate the reminders.
- We track renewal dates.
- We help you document cancellation friction.
- We help you spot patterns in companies that make cancellation difficult.
- We keep your subscription life organized, clear and protected.

You stay in control of your information.

We stay in service of your protection.

Why Subscription Watch is Different

⭐ We Don't Cancel Subscriptions For You - And That's On Purpose

Apps that "cancel for you" often require:

- full access to your inbox
- access your bank account
- permission to act on your behalf
- legal authorization to impersonate you

Subscription Watch™ doesn't do any of that.

Instead, we give you:

- step-by-step cancellation guidance
- friction ratings
- scripts
- documentation tools
- complaint pathways
- renewal alerts
- accountability tools

You keep your identity.
You keep your authority.
You keep your privacy.

⭐ Why This Matters

In a world where nearly every app wants access to your personal data, Subscription Watch™ **stands apart.**

We don't want your inbox.
We don't want your bank account.
We don't want your financial footprint.

We want you to feel **safe, informed,** and **in control.**

Subscription Watch™ is the subscription tool for people who refuse to give up their privacy just to stay organized.

Why Subscription Watch is Different

⭐ Comparison Snapshot

You deserve simple.

FEATURE	Subscription Watch™	Other Subscription Apps
Email Access Required	No	Yes - inbox scanning
Bank Access Required	No	Yes - transaction monitoring
Privacy First	Always	Rarely
Manual Entry	Yes - Intentional Control	No - automated scraping
Cancels Subscriptions	No - protects your identity	Yes - often requires impersonation
Tracks Renewal Dates	No - protects your identity	Yes
Free Trial Protection	Yes	Yes
Cancellation Friction Rating	Yes - unique feature	No
FTC Complaint Tools	Yes - built in	No
Data Collection	Minimal	Extensive

Intentionally Blank

Subscription revenue has grown 435% in the last decade.

Appendix

Speak louder than the chaos!

FTC Complaint Guide + Useful Scripts

You're in control now

How to File an FTC Complaint (Step-by-Step)

1. Visit reportfraud.ftc.gov

This is the official portal for reporting consumer fraud to the Federal Trade Commission (FTC). The service is complimentary, takes approximately five minutes to complete, and ensures that your report is reviewed.

2. Select Your Category

From the menu, choose either "Unwanted or Deceptive Charges" or "Subscription Trap."

3. Describe the events that transpired.

Please be specific: include dates, amounts, the actions you attempted, and the outcomes. Additionally, provide the company name and its URL.

4. Submit Your Evidence**

Upload any relevant documentation, including screenshots, statements, and emails. Include all materials that substantiate the basis of your complaint.

5. Submit and save your confirmation.

Upon submission, you will receive a reference number. It is important to retain this number, as the FTC may reach out to you in the event of an investigation.

⭐ Quick Reference Chart: Useful Resources

RESOURCE	WHAT IT DOES	WHY IT MATTERS	BEST FOR
FTC	Handles consumer complaints	Central authority for deceptive practices	Anyone filing a complaint
CFPB	Handles billing disputes	Protects against unauthorized charges	Surprise renewals
PRIVACY.COM	Virtual cards & spending limits	Prevents future traps	Free trials & risky merchants
DoNotPay	Automated cancellations & disputes	Saves time	Automation lovers
Billshark	Bill negotiation	Convenience	Lowering monthly costs
Subscription Watch (tm)	**Tracks & rates subscriptions**	**Your companion tool**	**Every reader**

SCAN
TO ACCESS YOUR TOOLS

Subscription Watch - FREE Access
Track subscriptions, rate friction, and stay ahead of surprise renewals.

swatch.voicesforsafety.com

FTC Complaint Assistant - Report deceptive cancellation practices.

https://ftc.gov

Consumer Financial Protection Bureau - Billing Complaint Portal - Dispute unauthorized charges.

https://www.consumerfinance.gov

PRIVACY.com - Virtual Cards - Prevent future traps

https://www.privacy.com

DoNotPay - Automation Tools - Automate cancellations and disputes.

https://donotpay.com

BILLSHARK - Negotiation Service - Lower bills with help.

https://www.billshark.com

FREE ACCESS

one reader

One Account

As the buyer of **The Subscription** Trap, you receive one free **Subscription Watch** account using the exclusive coupon code **SWATCHBOOK2026**

(valid until 12/31/2026)

That is a $9.99 SAVINGS

This code is valid for a single redemption and is intended only for the person who purchased this book. **Subscription Watch**™ is built on a privacy-first promise: We do not scan your email. We do not access your bank account. We do not monitor your financial life.

Your free access includes all core features, but it is limited to one account per reader. This protects the integrity of the system and ensures that every legitimate book owner receives the full benefit of the companion tool.

Subscription Watch™ - the subscription app that doesn't spy on you.

A final WORD

You're not losing your marbles for wanting a play-by-play of what you're being billed for. And you're certainly not a drama queen for thinking canceling should be as easy as pie. *You're a consumer with superpowers use them*!

If this guidebook helped you uncover a sneaky charge, *mission accomplished*! And I'm doing a ***happy dance***. Pass it on to someone else who could use a hand. We've got each other's backs when we spill the beans.

Wendy

www.ingramcontent.com/pod-product-compliance
Lightning Source LLC
LaVergne TN
LVHW051932051126
851857LV00020B/2083
* 9 7 9 8 2 3 4 1 8 8 2 2 9 *